30 DAYS

with

PAPA

*A simple journey deep into the heart
of the God you really want to know*

TOM WYMORE

*To Helen,
Lamentations 3: 21-23
Tom
Ps 27:4*

Editing, typesetting: Sally Hanan of Inksnatcher.com
Cover photo: 123rf.com/profile_lightfieldstudios

Ordering Information:
Quantity sales. Special discounts are available on quantity purchases by corporations, associations, and others. For details, contact Tom via email at tawymore@yahoo.com.

Note: 50 percent of all profits from this book will go to the following types of ministries: Christian orphanages in developing nations, ministries effectively working to end human trafficking, pro-life ministries, etc.

30 Days with Papa: A simple journey deep into the heart of the God you really want to know/Tom Wymore

ISBN 9781700108685

To Papa God, fierce and unrelenting in his pursuit of my heart, and my amazing wife, Charlie, radiant with Papa's love and joy

CONTENTS

As the Journey Begins

A Word Beforehand

You were created for intimacy with the God of the universe! Genesis 1:26–31 tells us that God created us to be caregivers for the earth and its creatures, but we are destined for far more than being mere caretakers. Because we are created in God's image, we have a built-in capacity for intimate relationship with our Creator. Consider the following:

In Genesis 3:8–9, we read that as God was walking in the garden in the cool of the day, he called out to his missing companions, Adam and Eve, "Where are you?" Since God certainly knew where they were and why they were hiding, why did he ask this question? Because he wanted *them* to know that he valued his relationship with them. He missed his intimate conversations with them!

Later in Genesis, Enoch is highlighted as a man who walked so intimately with God that God snatched him from the earth to enjoy perfect intimacy with him (5:1–24). We see the same relationship with God theme throughout the Old Testament. Abraham is described as God's friend. Moses had a face-to-face relationship with God. David passionately cried out for deep relationship with God, as seen in Psalms 27 and 63. Other psalmists had a similar passion, such as the sons of Korah (Psalm 42).

i

The New Testament makes it even clearer that we are created to live in intimate relationship with Papa God. Jesus modeled intimacy with his Father. Jesus stated often that his mission was to restore the relationship between people and his Father, and the apostle Paul described his core purpose in life as living in intimacy with Jesus (see Philippians 3:10–14). Paul also told us that Father God's purpose in Christ was to reconcile the world to himself (2 Corinthians 5:18–21).

So we were made for intimacy with God! Think about this for a moment, and you will be overwhelmed with awe. We tiny creatures are capable of, and destined for, intimate relationship with the infinite One. And the infinitely loving One paid an infinite price to make this possible. What wonder is this!

And no matter how well we know him, there's still all of our infinite God left to get to know. Deeper intimacy with God is *always* possible for *all* his people *all* the time. This thirty-day journey is meant to give you a fresh look into the heart of Father God ("Papa" to me), often by means of reflections from my own encounters with him.

Why a journey with Papa (Father God)? Some believers find it easier to relate to Jesus, or even Holy Spirit, than the Father, but this journey is deliberately focused on Papa. Why? Primarily because Jesus said that his goal was for his disciples to come to know the Father as he did (see John

14:6–10, 21–23; 16:25–28, etc.). Second, many of us need the healing and encouragement that a father must bring. This especially true for those of us who grew up with father wounds, but we *all* need to know God as Father more intimately. My own journey with God started with my being able to relate deeply only to Jesus (too much "father pain"), then progressed into a season of getting to know Holy Spirit (wow!), and eventually moved to the amazing place of intimacy with my Abba. So the journey we take for these is a journey of thirty days with Papa. My hope is that you will emerge from this simple journey drenched in his Father love and shaped by deep encounters with him.

ENTERING INTO INTIMACY

SOME SUGGESTED FIRST STEPS

Before we begin the actual journey, I offer a few thoughts on how to live in intimacy with God. My wife, Charlie, and I minister to a lot of people who have been believers for a long time but don't really know how to live intimately with God. So, just to make sure you have the basics down, I offer the following suggestions:

Commit to honesty.

This was a real key for me! Intimacy began for me partly because I stopped pretending that I was experiencing it. It's important for us to stop pretending or assuming that our lives and experiences match the intimacy with God we see in Scripture. It's safe to be completely honest with ourselves and God in the context of his grace and love, my friends. So instead of living in denial or feeling like you are defective, ask God to harmonize your life with his Word. Many believers unconsciously rewrite God's Word to match their experiences. Don't do that! When there is disagreement between experience and Scripture, rather than ignore it, ask God to change you. How does your life match up with the following Scriptures? (Look them up!)

- PSALM 34:8 How good does God "taste"?
- PSALM 63:1–3 Are you this desperate? Do you feel this loved?
- ROMANS 5:5; 8:14–17 Has his love inundated you? Does your heart cry out to him, "Daddy!"?
- ROMANS 14:17 How are your joy and peace levels? How about righteousness?
- GALATIANS 5:22–23 What usually comes out when someone bumps up against you?
- EPHESIANS 1:13–14 Is your experience of the Holy Spirit like a foretaste of heaven?

- 1 Corinthians 4:20 Is your experience of the kingdom of God one of just talk or supernatural power?

So how did you do? If there's a wide gap between your experience and verses like these, let it become not a rebuke but an invitation to do whatever it takes to know Papa intimately.

Be sure you get off to a good start.

All New Testament believers heard the gospel of the kingdom, not a gospel of the church or a gospel of getting saved from hell. That means that they had entered the family of God and experienced the following. They had:

- been unmistakably born from above (born again) through repentance and deep, total trust in Jesus.

- confessed Jesus as Lord, the complete master of their life.

- been baptized in water as a means of identification with Jesus and his family.

- been inundated by God's Spirit (baptized in the Spirit). Saturation and an unmistakable encounter with love and power through the Holy Spirit was the norm for every New Testament believer.

- undergone a process of inner healing and spiritual cleansing via deliverance, as needed.

Hunger for experience, not just ideas.

You can't be intimate with an idea. You can't cuddle up with a concept. Virtually every major Bible character became acquainted with God by means of an undeniable encounter with him. Check out some of Abraham's encounters (Genesis 12:1-9,13:14-17, 15:1-19). Remember Moses's introduction to God (Exodus 3). The list can go on and on. Many of us, though, were taught to fear or minimize experiences. How strange that would sound to Enoch, Moses, Gideon, David, Ezekiel, Paul, or Peter. The hunger part is important too. Passionate longing is what is described in the psalms mentioned earlier: "O God of my life, I'm lovesick for you in this weary wilderness. I thirst with the deepest longings to love you more, with cravings in my heart that can't be described. Such yearning grips my soul for you, my God!" (Psalm 63:1 TPT).

Find some spiritual friends.

My journey into intimacy really started via an impartation from Leslie Keegel, a humble Sri Lankan man who lives in amazing intimacy with Papa. Mentors can come from the past via books (Andrew Murray, A. W. Tozer, Brother Lawrence, et al.) or can be current friends who walk in intimacy with Jesus.

Make the relationship "normal"!

A relationship with God is more important than any human relationship and certainly has some major differences (!), but the things that build it are similar. Some people treat relationship with God in a way that would be weird for any human relationship. Ask yourself, "If I treated my relationship with _____ the way I treat my relationship with God, what would they think?" Healthy relationships are fun, filled with laughter as well as tears, spontaneous, never routine (lots of variety), and built by communication that includes both listening and talking. Does your relationship with God look like that? If not, consider rethinking your walk with God to make it look more "human."

But now, let's begin our journey.

WHAT IS PAPA REALLY LIKE?

What is God really like? How we view God, how we experience and think of him, greatly influences how we live out our lives with God. In his book *The Best of A. W. Tozer, Book One*, (Pennsylvania: WingSpread, 2007, 120), Tozer says: "Satan's first attack upon the human race was his sly effort to destroy Eve's confidence in the kindness of God. Unfortunately for her and for us he succeeded too well. From that day, men have had a false conception of God, and it is exactly this that has cut out from under them the ground of righteousness and driven them to reckless and destructive living." He later adds:

It is most important to our spiritual welfare that we hold in our minds always a right conception of God. If we think of him as cold and exacting, we shall find it impossible to love him, and our lives will be ridden with servile fear. If, again, we hold him to be kind and understanding, our whole inner life will mirror that idea. The truth is that God is the most winsome of all beings and his service one of unspeakable pleasure. He is all love, and those who trust him need never know anything but that love. Tozer's language is dated, but the truth of his words will never fade. So we start our journey with Papa by asking, "Who are you, Papa? What are you really like?"

1 WHAT IS PAPA LIKE?

Anyone who has seen me has seen the Father.
— John 14:9

What *is* God the Father (Papa) like? To me, the first and best answer is that God is like Jesus. Jesus clearly said that he is the perfect expression of the nature and heart of the Father. And Hebrews 1:3 says that Jesus, the Son of God, is the "exact representation of [God's] being." So when someone tells me s/he wants to know what God is like, I often suggest reading the Gospels over and over, asking, *What is Jesus really like?*

Think of the implications of this. Every action in Jesus's life and every word he spoke perfectly represent his Father. When we see Jesus's compassion breaking down every barrier to touch and cleanse a leper, we see the Father's compassion for outcast and marginalized people. When we see Jesus defend and save the woman caught in the act of adultery, we see Papa's mercy and compassion. (Imagine what she was feeling as she was dragged into Jesus's presence, expecting the worst!) When we see Jesus test the faith of the Phoenician woman, we know that Papa will not hesitate to call forth every ounce of faith he sees in us (even if we don't know it's there). When we see Jesus heal those who struggle to have any faith at all, we see Papa's heart to meet us at whatever point our faith is able to take us. Yes, if you see Jesus, you see the Father. There is absolutely no disagreement between who God Almighty, Maker of all things, is and who we meet and experience in Jesus.

May you, my friend, experience fresh wonder as you read the Gospels with an awareness that you

are seeing the very heart of the Father. And may
the wonder of your discoveries lead you into fresh,
new encounters with Papa God.

Response

All of us at various times can identify with those
who encountered Jesus. Why not look at a few of
the Gospel stories of people who encountered
Jesus, and put yourself in the story today? Keep in
your mind that you are encountering God: Father
and Son and Holy Spirit, as you do so. A few
suggestions are:

- What would it have been like to be the
  leper who wasn't sure Jesus was willing to
  heal him (Mark 1:40–45)? As you place
  yourself in the story as this man, what do
  you learn about what God is like? How does
  what you learn change your view of God,
  your perspective about life, and change you?

- Put yourself in the audience of those who
  heard the three parables Jesus told about
  God's heart for the lost (Luke 15). Switch
  roles in your imagination (Pharisees,
  "sinners" Jesus was defending, one of the
  disciples, etc.), and see how that changes
  things. Allow yourself to encounter Papa as
  you hear and see with fresh ears and eyes.
  How does your encounter with God's heart
  for the lost change how you view those who
  oppose our Christian values? Does God

love the doctor who performs abortions, the president of Planned Parenthood, the atheistic professor who humiliates believers in class? Does God's heart ever change toward his wandering children? Consider, too, what kind of welcome you will receive from him as you return from your own wandering. He is always the welcoming Father.

NOTES

2 GOD IS LOVE (PART 1)

Love is patient, love is kind. It does not envy, it does not boast, it is not proud. It does not dishonor others, it is not self-seeking, it is not easily angered, it keeps no record of wrongs. Love does not delight in evil but rejoices with the truth. It always protects, always trusts, always hopes, always perseveres.
– 1 Corinthians 13:4–7

What is Papa like? He is the most loving, patient, kind, forgiving Being in the universe! Your best ideas of love, kindness, patience, and forgiveness fall completely short of what he is really like. *God is like the person he encourages us to be, only infinitely so.* The New Testament descriptions of how believers are to treat one another and how we are to communicate with one another—all of these descriptions reveal what God is like because they express his nature.

So when the Bible describes the fruit that God's Spirit produces in us (Galatians 5:22–23), it is describing the essence of God. God *is* the most loving, joyful, peaceful, patient, kind, good, faithful, gentle, and self-controlled Being in the universe. Is that the God you know? It can be. I strongly recommend using Galatians 5:22–23 as a grid for your thoughts about God. When you sense God saying something to you or about you, when you sense his instruction to do something, stop and ask *Is this kind? Does this bring peace?* It will help you not only to hear him well but to know him as he truly is.

Another powerful description of God's character is found in 1 Corinthians 13. Because "God is love" (1 John 4:16), the description of love in 1 Corinthians 13:4–7 is what God is like. Replacing the word "love" in 1 Corinthians 13:4–7 with "Papa" or "Jesus" will captivate you with its description of this amazing God who invites you to know him. Here are just a few lines to get you started: "Papa is patient, Papa is kind. Papa never dishonors others, Papa never acts selfishly, Papa keeps no record of wrongs, Papa never delights in evil but always finds joy in and with the truth. Papa always protects, always trusts, always gives hope because he is an endless supply of hope that never gives up."

What is God like? He is the *infinite* expression of all the good things he instructs and empowers us to become. In the days ahead, we will continue to unfold the beauty of what God is like. For today, I trust your encounter with the kindest and most joyful being in the universe will touch the deepest parts of your life.

Response

Place God's name in *The Passion Translation*'s rendering of these verses and reflect deeply on what each one means for you now and in the future. Ask yourself if this is the God you know and are relating to. Ask God to shift your perception and experience of him to match the truth contained in these verses.

> Love is large and incredibly patient. Love is gentle and consistently kind to all. It refuses to be jealous when blessing comes to someone else. Love does not brag about one's achievements nor inflate its own importance. Love does not traffic in shame and disrespect, nor selfishly seek its own honor. Love is not easily irritated or quick

9

to take offense. Love joyfully celebrates honesty and finds no delight in what is wrong. Love is a safe place of shelter, for it never stops believing the best for others. Love never takes failure as defeat, for it never gives up.

– 1 Corinthians 13:4–7 TPT

The Passion Translation Bible

NOTES

3 GOD IS LOVE (PART 2)

God showed how much he loved us by
having Christ die for us, even though we
were sinful.
– Romans 5:8 CEV

Does God really *love* me? This question seems to hang in the back of the mind of everyone, believer and pre-believer (unbeliever today) alike. Yes, even self-described unbelievers, when they have their agnostic moments, catch themselves wondering if God loves them.

Does God, for sure, *really* love *you?* This question is often correctly answered by our pointing to the cross of Jesus. I add to this with what may be a new thought for you about how much Papa loves us. See if it speaks to you like it does to me.

The New Testament has only one recorded place where Jesus refers to his Father as "Abba" (which, as many of you know, is the equivalent of our "Papa" or "Daddy"). It's found in Jesus's prayer in the garden of Gethsemane (Mark 14:36). Jesus almost certainly used "Abba" often, but how important is it that the one place this is *recorded* is during his appeal to his Father in the garden? There, when Jesus was terrified of what he was facing, he called out to his Father as Abba's little boy. He asked his daddy if it were possible to take away the awful cup of suffering that was in front of him: "Papa, everything is possible for you. Please take this cup from me. Yet I will choose what you want, not what I want."

Does God really love you? God's answer is found written in the bloodstained, sweat-drenched soil of the garden of Gethsemane, as well on the cross. There in the garden we see a dearly loved son calling out to his daddy, using the tenderest word possible: "Abba." There has never been, in all history, a prayer that Father God *wanted* to say yes to more than this prayer! But he didn't. Why? Because of his great love for *you*. No one loves Jesus more than God the Father. And yet despite this great love for his son, the Father chose to say no to Jesus's appeal. Some might say it was easy for God to say no to the prayer of Jesus in Gethsemane because he knew the outcome. But such thinking greatly underestimates the infinite price that God the Son *and* God the Father paid to demonstrate their love. Knowing the outcome did not in *any* way diminish the "daddy pain" of the most loving Father for his most beloved Son as he suffered!

Today, any time you hear a child say "Daddy" or "Papa," remember Jesus in the garden of Gethsemane, intimately calling out to his Father, "Daddy, please take this cup from me!" Then remember that because of his great love for you, the prayer that the Father most wanted to answer with a yes was answered with "No!" because he loves *you*.

Response

Are you thinking that this is all well and good for everyone else but that God doesn't really love *you*? People often hear me say they are not the great cosmic exception! There are no exception clauses in the Bible's description of Papa's love. Now that we have established that, take some time and ask Holy Spirit to help you to complete a list of responses to the following statements.

BECAUSE GOD LOVES ME INFINITELY AND SPECIFICALLY AND IN A SPECIAL WAY . . .

- I am _____ (list several)
- I can _____ (list several)
- I will _____ (list several)
- I _____ (Make up your own!)

NOTES

4 GOD IS LOVE (PART 3)

Are not two sparrows sold for a penny?
Yet not one of them will fall to the ground
outside your Father's care. And even the
very hairs of your head are all numbered.
So don't be afraid; you are worth more
than many sparrows.
– Matthew 10:29–31

DAY 4

Did you know that you are God's favorite and that he loves you in a special way unique to you? Jesus's words make it obvious that Papa's love for you is specific and unique. We aren't the first to realize this remarkable truth, of course, but I was surprised that even hundreds of years ago there were some who knew that God loved them in a special way. Let me introduce you to two people who, though they lived long ago, help us understand that you and I are each Papa's favorite.

Brother Lawrence, a Carmelite lay brother who lived over three hundred years ago, experienced God's affection for him in a special way:

> I consider myself as the most wretched of men, full of sores and corruption, and who has committed all sorts of crimes against his King; touched with a sensible regret I confess to him all my wickedness, I ask his forgiveness, I abandon myself in his hands, that he may do what he pleases with me.

> This King, full of mercy and goodness, very far from chastising me, embraces me with love, makes me eat at his table, serves me with his own hands, gives me the key of his treasures; he converses and delights himself with me incessantly, in a thousand and a thousand ways, and treats me in all respects as his favorite. It is thus I consider myself from time to time in his holy presence.

Are you smiling yet? I wept and smiled the first time I read those words in Brother Lawrence's *The Practice of the Presence of God* (New York: Revell, 1895, 25). The thought of this simple, humble man from so long ago feeling like God's favorite just makes me smile!

But now let me introduce you to a believer who discovered God's affectionate, personalized love before Brother Lawrence was even born: Lady Julian of Norwich. Lady Julian was born in 1342. That's quite a while ago, isn't it? But listen to just a few quotes from her, and see if you catch her deep experience of God's customized love (Amy Laura Hall, *Laughing at the Devil: Seeing the World with Julian of Norwich* [Durham: Duke University Press, 2018, 124]):

> Love is nearest to us all. And this is the knowledge of which we are most ignorant; for many men and women believe that God is almighty and has power to do everything, and that he is all wisdom and knows how to do everything, but that he is all love and is *willing* to do everything—there they stop. And this ignorance is what hinders those who most love God; for when they begin to hate sin, and to mend their ways . . . there still remains some fear which moves them to think of themselves and their previous sins. And they take this fear for humility, but it is foul ignorance and weakness. . . . for *it comes from the Enemy, and it is contrary to Truth. . . .*

19

> It is God's wish that we should place most
> reliance on *liking* and *love*; for it makes
> God's power and wisdom very gentle to us;
> just as through his generosity God forgives
> our sins when we repent, so he wants us to
> forget our sins and all our depression and
> all our doubtful fear.
>
> – emphasis mine

Pretty amazing? And there are many others throughout history, even in its darkest periods, who lived in God's affectionate embrace. Religion, with its suffocating bent toward performance, always squelches the power and simplicity of living in Papa's embrace. But there has always been a witness, a soft but beautiful light, of God's personal, special love for each of us rising from the dark swamp of the religion of Christianity.

Response

"Look with wonder at the depth of the Father's marvelous love that he has lavished on us! He has called us and made us his very own beloved children" (1 John 3:1 TPT). Take some time today to stop and consider whether you consistently feel like you are God's favorite. Does that thought make you squirm? If so, ask Papa why and what he wants to say about it. Also, make a list of what God likes about you and share it with a trusted friend.

NOTES

5 PAPA IS PATIENT IN HIS LOVE

His Mercy is New everyday *God (Hebrew)*

In my mind I keep returning to something, something that gives me hope—that the grace of Adonai is not exhausted, that his compassion has not ended. [On the contrary,] they are new every morning! How great your faithfulness!

– Lamentations 3:21–23 CJB

Do you ever run out of patience with yourself?
Maybe I'm the only one who does that, but I am
truly glad that God *never* runs out of patience with
us.

I am not sure why God's unending patience is
so hard for me to grasp. I have written many words
about it, but I still tend to forget that God's basic
nature is patient love: patient, unfailing, endless
commitment to do what is best for you and me.

I smile as I write this, though, because God's
patience with us is why he keeps patiently
reminding us that he is patient. God's love for us is
why he keeps reminding us and showing us (in
thousands of ways) that he loves us. What a
beautiful situation we are in. No matter which way
we turn, we run into his patience and love!

But is his patience with us permission to take
advantage of him or to continue to wallow in self
focus or do harmful things? Of course not. God's
love for us leads us away from such things into
transformation. His love also gives us the power to
get there (both in choosing and in doing). His
patience assures us that we can always run to him,
no matter what. Father knows that he alone is our
refuge, he alone can lead us to wholeness and
purposeful living. He alone gives fruitfulness and
life, not as some heavenly Santa Claus but as a
loving parent who guides his children to a mature
partnership in his purposes. So he will pursue us
with his patience and chase us down with his love—

not to make things magically easy but to return us, again and again, into the sphere of his powerful, transforming love.

Do you need a reminder of Papa's *patient* love for you today? Personally, I sometimes feel I am still a toddler in terms of intimacy with him. But when I feel like that, I find that if I lean on his patience, I won't become discouraged and disabled in my quest to know him. Perhaps that's why he has so often reminded me of the golden strand of his goodness. Let me invite you into the inner sanctuary of my heart as Papa and I conversed about this a while back. Perhaps something in our conversation will speak to you as well. I close with this excerpt from my 2012 journal:

I am making progress, Papa, as you lead and shape me. Forgive me for complaining along the way. I suppose I would do that less if I would just let you love me. I realized afresh this morning (or was it last night?) how little I truly understand about intimacy with you and how I have tended to view even the journey into intimacy as a series of things to be checked off a list! Show me your ways, bring me into your heart, I pray, Papa. I can't even understand this and certainly can't live this unless you aid me all along the way.

"It's not that hard, little one. Just keep listening and allowing me to love you! I won't lose track of you, nor will I run out of love and patience."

Ah, Father. That last line especially gets to me: you never run out of patience! I need to remember that I Corinthians 13:4-7 really is a description of who you always are.

– Tom's journal, December 28, 2012

Response

Do you ever run out of patience with yourself? Do you ever catch yourself thinking that God probably does too? What would your life look like if you were as patient (but also as firm) with yourself as God is? Reflect on this for few minutes, remembering that God's patience with us is not permission to fail but forgiveness and encouragement when we do. Need to be sure your slate is clean? Ask his forgiveness, but then move quickly back into his embrace, listening for his encouragement as well as his instruction.

NOTES

.

6 PAPA IS KIND

Don't you see how wonderfully kind,
tolerant, and patient God is with you?
Does this mean nothing to you? Can't
you see that his kindness is intended to
turn you from your sin?
— Romans 2:4 NLT

What is God like? Graham Cooke often says God is the kindest Being in the universe, and we touched on this thought earlier. A personal story from my life clearly illustrates this.

The time of testing I experienced during my first wife's battle with cancer provided me with overwhelming evidence that God is kind beyond belief! Papa's kindness extends to the tiniest details of our lives, with subtle nuances and loving touches that cause us to bow in stunned worship. Let me illustrate this via a couple of touches that Papa gave to me during the battle.

As you can imagine, my first wife's battle caused me to be the target for repeated attacks designed to create fear in me. Those attacks frequently succeeded so that I would find myself fearfully crying out to God while also clinging to one of my theme verses: "Whenever I am afraid, I will trust in (lean into, lean upon) You" (Psalm 56:3 NKJV). Two of God's responses to those desperate cries clearly reveal his kind attention to detail.

The first occurred one night after I had gone to bed, wrestling with various fears. After falling into fitful sleep, I rolled over in the middle of the night and glanced at the clock, which read 3:57. As soon as I saw those numbers, I heard Papa whisper, "Mark that time." So I did just that, marking those numbers in my mind. In the morning, I realized that it probably pointed to a Bible verse, but I assumed it would point to something like 35:7.

Surely there are no chapters that long in the Bible, I thought. but as I began my search for a meaningful 35:7 (Psalms, Isaiah, etc.), I heard Papa say, "No, look at 3:57!" So I did a quick search, not really confident that I was hearing God at that point. To my amazement, I discovered one 3:57 in the Bible, in Lamentations of all places! *This can't be good,* I thought; *it's in Lamentations!* But then I read it: "You came near when I called you, and you said, 'Do not fear.'" I was stunned and began weeping, not only because of the spot-on words but because of my wonder at God orchestrating so many things to speak directly to my fears. And as I wept, I felt his smile.

The second incident is described in this journal entry from November 17, 2009:

> Ah, Father, you take me to the Smith Wigglesworth devotional *not* to read the entry (although it was good) but to remind me of the Ellel bookmark there with the picture I noticed the other day of a young man holding his baby aloft!
>
> "Yes, little one, so precious to me; *you* are the child, I AM the Father. Ponder that, my beloved!"
>
> Oh, Father! As I look back at Isaiah 63:9, I see the rest of the verse! "In his love and mercy he redeemed them. *He lifted them up*

and carried them through all the years" (NLT). And then you have me look again at the love-locked gaze between father and child, and then at the pictures on my blog where my gaze is lovingly locked on my sons. Ah, Papa! Thank you for reminding me, in ways beyond comprehension, what it looks like to 'live in the Father's affection.' You are an infinitely better and more loving father than I ever could be, and yet . . . I am so undone!

I hope you don't find these experiences too mystical. They are two of thousands that happen all the time to God's children as they learn to live loved and listening. For those who have eyes to see and ears to hear, God is always kind, always speaking, always encouraging, always expressing his love in remarkably consistent and precise ways. And these to me are part of the answer to the question *What is God like?* He is the kindest Being in the universe!

Response

Pause today to consider some of the ways you have experienced God's kindness in your life. Remember that his kindness expands far beyond conversations with him like the ones I described above. God's kindness comes through others, through events, through the Bible. Yes, thank him for specific expressions of his kindness before leaving this time with Papa!

NOTES

7 PAPA'S KINDNESS AND OUR FAITH

*Be kind and compassionate to one
another, giving grace to one another, just
as God in Christ has showered grace
upon you.*
– Ephesians 4:32 (my paraphrase)

Here's another reflection on God's kindness and what it looks like, specifically how God's kindness relates to our trust in him.

Many years ago, I heard one of my scoutmasters say that he taught his sons to swim by taking them to the end of a fishing dock and throwing them into the deep water (really!). He was kind of proud of this, but I remember wondering if he was very safe! I didn't really feel like he was someone I could trust. How about you?

Is trust developed by putting people into frightening situations? In other words, if I wanted my sons to learn to trust me, would I do that by placing them into a situation that would scare them to death? Wouldn't it be more likely that if I wanted my sons to trust me, I would be kind and gentle, rescuing them as needed from anything harmful while also teaching them how to face tough things maturely? I would do this not by sink or swim but by getting into the water with them! It seems to me that trust grows when someone is good to us, not when they deliberately set us up for hard things.

What's my point? Simply that I sometimes tend to think that God puts me into hard situations to "make" me have faith. After all, since he "allowed" this hard thing, he must be expecting me to grow in faith through it. The problem with this kind of thinking, though, is that it makes me less likely to trust God or get close to him. Furthermore, this thinking is simply not biblical. Scripture does tell us that trouble, trials, and tribulation will come, but my Bible tells me that this is so that my faith can be tested and revealed (1 Peter 1:6–7). Yes, sometimes this testing takes us beyond where we think we can go, but this is to reveal that God can be relied on, not to force us to rely on him with a faith that isn't there (2 Corinthians 1:8–11). Rather, the faith that is already in us because of our past experiences of God's faithfulness rises up and surprises us with its presence! This is not true, though, for people who believe faith is a feeling. Faith is not a feeling. <u>Fear is a feeling.</u> <u>Faith is a settled decision to trust, even in the dark</u>, not blindly but boldly, because we know who God really is—and he is really, really kind.

It seems to me that if I am to grow in my trust of God (or anyone), my trust will grow most by a revelation of that person's goodness, love, and trustworthiness, not by my having to trust him or her because I have no other choice. Thank you, Papa, for your kind compassion, which leads us to trust you.

Response

Take a moment to think about what you have been taught about faith. Does it make it sound more like God is kind or cruel (like the scoutmaster)? What changes need to happen in your thinking about faith in light of this teaching about God's kindness?

Day 7

How will you view troubles and challenges in the future given this insight? What other reflections, thoughts, or feelings are happening in you right now? Write a few of them down for later consideration.

NOTES

8 Papa Is Tender and Merciful

Remember, O Lord, Your tender mercies
and Your lovingkindnesses, for they are
from of old.
— Psalm 25:6 NKJV

Shortly after my first wife, Jettie, died, I was, of course, deep in the throes of grief, hurting beyond description, unable to see anything other than the ruins of my life. I remember that for some reason, even though I was hurting that badly, I found myself expecting to hear God tell me to suck it up. I'm not sure why I thought that—I guess it's pretty much how I was raised—but whatever the reason, I was, instead, blown away by God's kindness and tender, relentless pursuit of my heart. At every point in my pain, he lovingly embraced me, no matter what my frame of mind or emotional state. Whether I was in the depths of despair, feeling like a miserable failure, or trying hard to be strong, I kept bumping into my Father's love. He was, and continues to be, infinitely patient and tender with me, and I am convinced that his tender-mercies approach is what brought me to my current state of strength and wholeness.

The following quote is from my journal on December 8, 2010, two months after Jettie died:

I keep expecting you to tell me to suck it up like my dad tended to do. Somehow it rarely occurs to me that you don't do that when someone is "bleeding all over the floor," or even that you would never, ever, do that to anyone. Do I think I am kinder than *you* are??? Where on earth did we get this notion that telling wounded people to be tough is best for them? Who would go to a doctor who gave that advice? And this is a wound far deeper than any physical wound.

But wait, you say! Surely there is a place for toughness and pressing in and on. Yes, of course there is, but timing and context determine how encouragement is to be given. God is perfectly attuned to where you are and to what your circumstances are, dear one. So when you are "bleeding all over the floor" because of tragedy, you will find his tender mercies inviting you to be healed, not cruelly telling you to get over it! When you are starting to recover but still walking with a limp, you will find his tender mercies urging you forward: "I am with you. Don't be afraid. Keep pressing on. In your weakness you will be made strong." And even when you are feeling on top of the world, you will discover his tender mercies! This time they will be there to remind you to live in gratitude and graciousness, to fiercely enjoy the feeling of the wind beneath your wings. Everywhere you turn, you'll find his tender mercies! It's not like he runs out of grace. His mercies are being renewed *every morning* (Lamentations 3:22–23).

I truly do wish that I could convey what's in my heart, what I have seen as I have peered into God's heart and seen his kindness. Yes, he will stretch us, challenge us, and exhort us, but I marvel at how he does all of this with such tender mercy!

Response

I trust you aren't getting bored by my repeated emphasis upon God's kindness. If I overemphasize these things, it's because I am attempting to overcome a mountain of false perceptions of our Papa. Feel free to push back, if you wish, by writing out your questions and objections. And if you have none, why not write your own list of times when you have been shocked by tender mercy? Yes, this truth about Papa is too good not to be true! Step into his mercies again today—they are made fresh and new today, just for you!

NOTES

9 PAPA IS GOOD, PERIOD!

*I will cause all my goodness to pass in
front of you.*
– Exodus 33:19

Your very best idea or experience of "good" falls totally short of how good God truly is. *God is good beyond comprehension.* God is *so* good that we will *never* fully experience all his goodness.

Even in the Old Testament, which makes some people think that God is a bit grouchy, he reveals himself as profoundly good. When Moses asked to see God's glory, God answered, "I will cause all my *goodness* to pass in front of you and proclaim my name, Yahweh, in your presence. I am having mercy on those on whom I am having mercy, and I am having compassion on those on whom I am having compassion" (Exodus 33:19, my paraphrase). The next day, when God caused his glory (goodness!) to pass by Moses, he said, "The Lord, the Lord, the compassionate and gracious God, slow to anger, abounding in love and faithfulness, maintaining love to thousands, and forgiving wickedness, rebellion and sin" (Exodus 34:6–7). "Compassionate and gracious, slow to anger, abounding in love" is God's own description of his very essence—amazing!

This same phrase is repeated in other places in the Old Testament, including Numbers 14:18, Psalm 86:15, Psalm 103:8, Joel 2:13, and Jonah 4:2, forming a golden strand of reminders of what God is really like: totally, infinitely good!

So, what do you think people who know God as he really is (good!) are like? What are people like who know they are treasured by a God who is compassionate and gracious, slow to anger, and rich in love? Remember, people become like the God they know and serve.

Response

Perhaps a better question is what is God like *to you?* The God who is love invites you to get to know him as he really is. Reflect today on what each of these words and phrases means to you personally: *compassionate, gracious, slow to anger, rich in love.* Take the time to really think about each one. It may change your life!

NOTES

10 Papa

Is a Father
Not an Inspector

*The Spirit you received does not make
you slaves, so that you live in fear
again; rather, the Spirit you received
brought about your adoption to
sonship. And by him we cry, "Abba,
Father."*
— Romans 8:15 NIV

When God asks you a question, do you hear an invitation or an accusation? I have been thinking about how easy it is to put a negative spin on the questions God asks me (or people in the Bible). For example, when I hear, "Why are you afraid?" I may think, because of my fear, God is saying I am defective, rather than him inviting me to trust him. Or "Where is your faith?" may sound like an accusation about unbelief instead of an invitation to explore God's love and power to increase my trust. You get the picture.

I think that we tend to put a negative spin on what God says because we still very much need our paradigms adjusted in terms of who God is and what he is really like to his children. Reviewing the following words by Andrew Murray, from *With Christ in the School of Prayer* (New York: Fleming H. Revell, 1895, emphasis added), often helps me return to a healthier understanding of who God is. He is not our heavenly inspector, he is our loving Father! See what you think:

> We are afraid to take God as our tender Father. We think of him as a schoolmaster or an inspector, who knows nothing about us except through our lessons. . . . We aren't supposed to learn to be holy as a hard lesson at school so we can make God think well of us. We are to learn it at home with the Father to help us. God loves you not because you are clever or good, but because He is *your Father.* The cross of Christ does not *make* God love us. It is the *outcome* of

His love to us. His love lies underneath
everything. We must grasp it as the solid
foundation of our religious life, not
growing up *into* that love, but growing
up *out of it.*

*We are to begin in the patient love of our
Father.* Think about how He knows us
personally, as individuals with all our
peculiarities, our weaknesses, and our
difficulties. The master judges by the result,
but our Father judges by the effort.

Don't you love that last line? But please don't
read into it that God's first response to you is
judgment! The point is that God as Father is
always *for* us and not *against* us, *never* looking for
reasons to condemn us but *always* looking for
reasons to commend us. Will correction come? Yes,
but as it comes it brings hope and power to change
because he is our loving Father, not a heavenly
inspector!

Response

What do you think this wise old saint meant when
he said, "not growing up *into* that love but growing
up *out of it*"? To help you with this reflection,
consider Ephesians 3:17–19: "I pray that you, being
rooted and firmly established in love, may be able
to comprehend with all the saints what is the
length and width, height and depth of God's love,
and to know Christ's love that surpasses
knowledge, so that you may be filled with all the

fullness of God" (CSB). Take time to reflect on these verses until you can restate them in your own, personalized version of this passage.

NOTES

11 PAPA

LOVES THE LEAST AND THE LITTLE

Jesus said, "Let the little children come to me, and do not hinder them, for the kingdom of heaven belongs to such as these." When he had placed his hands on them, he went on from there.
— Matthew 19:14–15

She sat quietly with her mommy on the front row, a precious little girl who had known lots of trauma and sadness. Her mother had recently returned to the Lord with great zeal, but not before many men had inflicted wounds on this little child. Yet there she sat, quietly and peacefully coloring while I spoke. I could hear her softly whispering and softly singing to her mommy (it was so cute!).

Then, right in the middle of my lecture, I felt led to share a quote from the brilliant German theologian, Karl Barth. Someone had once asked him how he would summarize all his great theological works. This great thinker simply replied, "Jesus loves me, this I know, for the Bible tells me so." As I was sharing this story, the little girl's face lit up with wonder and joy, so much so that I asked her mother what was going on. To the amazement of the entire class, her mother revealed that at the very same moment I quoted Karl Barth, her little girl was singing "Jesus Loves Me"!

Suddenly, we all became deeply aware that God was incredibly present, and we were drawn into a wonderful moment of basking in God's "Father love." We may have sung the song—I can't remember—but I do remember the weight of God's presence filling the room with his goodness.

Later, as I reflected on that remarkable moment, I told God how grateful I was for his confirming what I was teaching. What followed was one of those gentle but life-changing corrections from

Papa. He said simply, "I didn't do that for you, Tom, nor for the class. I did it for the little girl!" And then I understood...and I wept, and I worshiped.

Do you understand? As you do, you will weep and worship as well.

Response

Take some time to reflect on the following passages and think about what Jesus's heart for children says about God, you, and our world. Consider picturing yourself as present in the stories and write down your thoughts.

> Then people brought little children to Jesus for him to place his hands on them and pray for them. But the disciples rebuked them.
>
> Jesus said, "Let the little children come to me, and do not hinder them, for the kingdom of heaven belongs to such as these." When he had placed his hands on them, he went on from there.
>
> – Matthew 19:13–15 NIV

> He called a little child to him, and placed the child among them. And he said: "Truly I tell you, unless you change and become like little children, you will never enter the kingdom of heaven. Therefore, whoever takes the lowly position of this child is the greatest in the kingdom of heaven."
>
> – Matthew 18:2–4 NIV

Notes

12 PAPA

EMBRACES

YOU IN THE DARKEST

VALLEY

*Lord, even when your path takes me
through the valley of deepest darkness,
fear will never conquer me, for you
already have! You remain close to me and
lead me through it all the way. . . . The
comfort of your love takes away my fear.
I'll never be lonely, for you are near.*
— Psalm 23:4 TPT

Mother's Day, May 9, 2010, was one of the very worst days of my life, because on that day my first wife, Jettie, was hospitalized for level 10 pain from the cancer eating away at her body. It was one of a string of days that were the worst days of my life, during Jettie's painful journey, beginning with her diagnosis of the inoperable tumor on August 12, 2009. The emotional impact of *that* worst day is still with me, bringing tears to my eyes as I write, almost ten years later. And that worst day was made even worse by my not being with her as she heard this grim diagnosis. I remember crumpling to the floor, sobbing uncontrollably, after I talked with her doctor by phone.

But God was there with us in those days in the darkest valley. I can't begin to describe the many ways we sensed Papa's presence and saw his hand in that long, dark time. But here are a few with you moments from my journal during that time.

On May 10, 2010, we drove to Denver for a procedure that severed some nerves in an attempt to lessen her pain, and revealed the progress of the disease. I recorded these words that day:

So many promises, Father. I cling to them and to you as best I can. Papa, you know all things, so you know it's the horror of watching Jettie in extreme pain that cuts me the most. This cannot be your perfect will, but like the father of the demonized

57

boy, all I can say is Lord, I believe. Help thou my unbelief!

May 11, 2010, 4:39 p.m. I wrote:

Papa, my foot is slipping again, and probably because I again allowed something to cause me to slip out of your hand. I know I shouldn't have read the medical report again, Papa. I am glad that we are home and that Jettie is making some slow progress, but she is terribly discouraged, Pai (Papa), and it's hard not to take that on. And so here I am, wanting to feel your touch, seeking your face, trying to quiet my heart. I think of Psalm 94:17-19 a lot these days, Pai, and I find it again as you lead me back six months, along with the truly appropriate Psalm 13. Ah, Father, only in looking at your face can we find strength and faith.

Is this too gloomy? Then consider this: In every instance, as I wrote these pain-filled words, Papa drew near to me and to my beloved bride. He would speak very clearly, cutting the heart out of our fears and replacing those fears with hope and peace. Even more amazing, after a series of prayer times that month, Jettie's pain diminished to the point of being totally manageable up until the day she died! The surgery didn't help, but the prayers of God's people did! She was actually cutting back on pain meds as she entered her final days!

May 16:

Papa: "Do you know yet, child, how to LIVE in my embrace? Then you have more to experience, and you have my invitation afresh to do so! Fly, eagle, into my love!"

Ah, Papa . . . It really is all about living loved and listening. The picture I had just now was of two lovers dancing, eyes locked on each other, not glancing away for a moment. It's in your loving embrace, where nothing else matters but you, looking with love at your face, that this life is meant to be lived out. You have shown me this many times, but only now is it being deepened.

So the walk through the darkest valley turns out to be a dance! The God who prepares a table in the presence of our enemies and comforts us with rod and staff also dances with us in the valley. No, it's not the joyful dance of victory but the dance of two lovers locked so tightly together that they move through the storm *more aware of one another than the storm.*

Response

Take some time with Papa and allow him to speak to your fears, worries, and concerns, listening for his answer. Perhaps you will hear him say, even in your valley, "May I have this dance?" Write down what you hear, and be sure to put today's date on it.

NOTES

13 PAPA

SHOUTS IN OUR PAIN

Unless the Lord had given me help, I would have soon dwelt in the silence of death. When I said, "My foot is slipping!" your unfailing love, Lord, supported me. When anxiety was great within me, your consolation brought joy to my soul.
— Psalm 94:17—19

Tom's note: The following article was written during the last part of the battle for Jettie's life (July 24, 2010). I have intentionally left the wording in the present tense to retain its impact.

It was C. S. Lewis who said that God shouts in our pains. That phrase has come to my mind again today, as it has many times in the past several months.

Today (July 24, 2010) I write more from a place of pain than anything else, yet I am amazed at how Papa is shouting to me. I have written about some of his "shouting" in past blogs (August 26 and November 20, 2009, and January 21, 2010), but each of the previous times I was writing from a better-looking place than what we are in right now. Yet Papa continues to shout encouragement to me, and I am totally undone by these expressions of his stubborn, pursuing love.

It may seem at times that God stops communicating when things get rough, or that he tends to whisper while our pain and the enemy are shouting. Thankfully, God not only shouts when the storms threaten to drown out his voice, he shouts at just the right time with just the right words! All we have to do is pay a wee bit more attention once we detect his shouts. Today, for example, everywhere I was looking, I was being reminded of key scriptural promises God has given to us. He was using glances at the clock, license plate numbers on the car in front of me, emails and Facebook comments, and more. I would have to be really out of touch not to hear him right now!

Isn't this what we expect a good parent to do? When healthy parents find unwanted noise threatening to drown out what their child needs to hear, they raise the volume and intensity of their words. The greater the danger and the larger the need, the louder and more persistent the communication is until the message gets through!

A child can choose to ignore his or her parent's shouts, but I for one don't want to do that, and I doubt that you do either. So today I come, listening as best I can, choosing to fix my gaze on the face of the one who is the speaking voice. Then his peace comes, his face begins to blot out the misperceptions, and his truth begins to replace "the facts" as I perceive them.

Thank you, Papa, for shouting today until you captured my attention. I long for the day when I can hear your whisper in the storm, but I am unspeakably grateful that, for now, you shout!

> If I say, 'My foot is slipping,'
> your faithful love will support me, Lord.
> When I am filled with cares,
> your comfort brings me joy.
>
> – Psalm 94:18–19 CSB

Response

One story in particular in the Gospels gives us a good picture of Jesus shouting in a storm. Can you think of it? Put yourself in the place of the disciples in the storm on the Sea of Galilee and imagine their emotions when they heard Jesus's voice above the storm (Matthew 14:22–33). Now reflect on times in your life when God has shouted in your pain. Why not take some time to thank him and renew your confidence in his future communications during the storms you are enduring or know will come?

NOTES

14 Papa Plans for Our Failures

But I have prayed for you, Simon, that your faith may not fail. And when you have turned back, strengthen your brothers.

— Luke 22:32

God seems to have a totally different view of failure than I do. He doesn't fear failure in you or me. In fact, he plans for it. A story from the life of Simon Peter, an accomplished "failer," helps us to see how God views failure.

Parts of this story about Peter's failure are well known, such as Peter's three-time denial of Jesus, but I want to focus on a lesser-known part of that story:

> "Simon, Simon! Satan has asked to sift all of you disciples like wheat. But I have prayed for you, Simon. I have prayed that your faith will not fail. When you have turned back, help your brothers to be strong."
>
> But Simon replied, "Lord, I am ready to go with you to prison and to death."
>
> Jesus answered, "I tell you, Peter, you will say three times that you don't know me. And you will do it before the rooster crows today."
>
> – Luke 22:31–34 NIV

Several things stand out in this story. First, Jesus was fully aware of the impending failure of all his disciples, and he prepared them for this by warning them and praying for Simon in particular. Wow! Did you catch that? Jesus was anticipating failure and praying about it before it happened. (This may give us a clue as to some of what he is praying for about us! See Romans 8:34). Second, Jesus views

failure differently than we typically do. Instead of
praying for Simon not to fail, he prayed that
Simon's *faith* would not fail. But Peter's faith did
fail, or so it seems, so what's up with that? My guess
is that Jesus views faith as a process, with bumps
and temporary failures along the way as part of the
faith package. In other words, he looks at the entire
picture and not just the occasional failures. I
wonder if he views our failures this way. (I think he
does!) Finally, Jesus is so unafraid of Simon's
failure that even while he was predicting it, he
called Simon by the special name he gave him
(Peter, which means *rock*). This is huge to me. Jesus
is saying, "You will fail, but you are still *a rock* in my
view." I wonder if that's how he views us? I think
he does.

Have you failed miserably? I have, more than
once. As I was writing this, I remembered how I
totally lost my temper while driving in a snowstorm
during my first wife's battle with cancer. Jettie had
to listen to me have a meltdown that culminated in
me ranting and raving about another driver. This is
extremely out of character for me (thankfully), but I
was appalled that I allowed fear to make me so
vulnerable to anger. But it's what Papa said about it
the next day that still blows me away and confirms
that he views failure very differently from how I
view it. Below are his words to me:

I am not disappointed in you, but rather, I
feel your fears, and like any good father, I

am grieved because of that which assaults you. Don't be afraid, little one. I am holding on to you and your beloved, and I will continue to hold on. Whenever your foot is slipping, my love will surely support you. Whenever you feel overwhelmed, I will be there in the midst of your pain and fear, holding on to you more tightly than you can imagine.

I was completely undone by these words. Instead of judging me during my anxious and angry moments, Papa was feeling the pain that brought me to that point, and he was in the midst of my failure even as it was happening. Yes, God's view of failure is very different from ours. And my prayer is that you will begin viewing yours differently from this day on!

Response

Are you holding on to some past failure that you need to release? My hope in writing this chapter is that the truth that God plans for our failures will enable you to release failure by forgiving yourself.

Perhaps, too, you may need to hand over to Papa any fear of failure that binds you. Confidence that he knows how to work even our failures out for our good enables us to live free from fear of future failure and take the risks that faith often requires!

NOTES

15 PAPA
LOVES YOU
EVEN IF YOU WHINE

My God, my God, why have you forsaken me? Why are you so far from saving me, so far from my cries of anguish? My God, I cry out by day, but you do not answer, by night, but I find no rest.
— Psalm 22:1–2

Does God love us when we whine? I hope so—whining is sprinkled throughout my journals! Thankfully, I know the psalmists also whined as part of a healthy relationship with Papa.

The psalmists teach us a lot through their complaints to the Lord. They show us that confidence in God's love gives us "freedom to whine." They teach us that God's desire for intimacy requires us to be transparent. What kind of relationship would we have if certain kinds of communication weren't allowed? They also remind us that since God knows everything (Psalm 139), it's silly to try to hide what God already knows. In addition to Psalm 22:1–2 above, consider the following examples of "healthy whining":

> Look at them—the wicked!
>
> They are always at ease,
>
> and they increase their wealth.
>
> Did I purify my heart
>
> and wash my hands in innocence for nothing?
>
> For I am afflicted all day long
>
> and punished every morning.
>
>   – Psalm 73:12–14 CSB

> My enemies have chased and caught me
>
> and crushed my life into dust.
>
> Now I'm living in the darkness of death's shadow.

> My inner being is in depression
> and my heart is heavy, dazed with despair.
>
> – Psalm 143:3–4 TPT

God doesn't love you less when you whine; instead, he invites you to pour out your pain to him. But the psalmists show us how to whine wisely. Look at the context of the verses I just quoted. "You are holy, enthroned on the praises of Israel. Our fathers trusted in you; they trusted, and you rescued them. They cried to you and were set free; they trusted in you and were not disgraced" (Psalm 22:3–5 CSB). David complained but also turned his focus to God and his faithfulness, alternating between complaint, appeal, and affirmation (throughout Psalm 22).

David said,

> I remember the days of old; I meditate on all you have done; I reflect on the work of your hands. I spread out my hands to you; I am like parched land before you. Answer me quickly, Lord; my spirit fails. Don't hide your face from me, or I will be like those going down to the Pit. Let me experience your faithful love in the morning, for I trust in you. Reveal to me the way I should go because I appeal to you.
>
> – Psalm 143:5–8 CSB

Again, David blended complaint and desperate appeal with a steady focus upon God and his faithfulness.

The psalmists show us that wise whining flows from an awareness of God's presence. We aren't screaming at the heavens, we are pouring out our pain to a Papa who is carefully listening. This enables us to move past our pain into reminders of God's goodness and finally into renewed hope and trust. The psalms of complaint inevitably end with a full declaration of renewed trust in the trustworthiness of God. Whining done in this manner leads us to experience Papa's perspective and Papa's embrace. We whine because of pain and fear, but awareness and declaration of his presence, his goodness, and his character lead us back into his perspective and into an encounter with his love and peace.

My friend, don't spiritualize your life to the point of not whining and thereby diminish your relationship with God. Whine wisely, starting with an awareness of God's presence, then move from complaint to remembering to affirming to declaration. This will deepen your relationship with Papa and lessen your whining over the long haul.

I close with this example from my journal, shortly after Jettie's death:

Ah, Father. I am so very wounded right now. I cannot bear the thought of ever fighting another battle. But I press on, plodding along, putting one foot in front of the other even as I know that you are holding on to me and catching my tears in your bottle of remembrance.

Response

Jeremiah's great lament is a powerful example of clinging to God while pouring out complaint. Jeremiah didn't know God as we can—he thought God was the source of his pain—but we can learn from his faith in the midst of pain. Consider Lamentations 3:21–33.

NOTES

16 Papa Encourages You with Grace and Compassion

Never let ugly or hateful words come from your mouth, but instead let your words become beautiful gifts that encourage others; do this by speaking words of grace to help them.
– Ephesians 4:29 TPT

Let no harmful language come from your mouth, only good words that are helpful in meeting the need, words that will benefit those who hear them.
– Ephesians 4:29 CJB

I said on day 2 that Papa is like the person he instructs us to be. I return to that thought today, because one of the most important areas this truth addresses is what God sounds like. What *does* God sound like? Does he sound like Ephesians 4:29 when he speaks to you? Perhaps he sounds more like a harsh or angry parent or a judgmental friend? No, Ephesians 4:29 and 1 Corinthians 14:3 tell us what Papa sounds like.

When the Bible tells us to use words that are "helpful for building others up according to their needs, that it may benefit those who listen" (Ephesians 4:29) and that strengthen, encourage, and comfort (1 Corinthians 14:3), it is indeed revealing what God sounds like when he speaks to us. When I first realized this, it opened up a brand-new level of relationship with Papa for me. I realized that my filters for God's words shut out much of his kindness and encouragement. God, to me at least, sounded a lot like a harsh parent. Now I know, both through Scripture and personal experience, that when God speaks, he encourages, comforts, and builds us up with grace and compassion.

I have already shared personal stories that illustrate this, but here is one more.

Many years ago, when I was about thirty-two years old, I was walking on the beach at Ebey's Landing in Whidbey Island, Washington, telling God what a miserable failure I was. I had, by my own foolish choices, hurt my closest friends and my wife and done great damage to the congregation I was pastoring. My sense of failure was great, and so I was persistently telling God what a miserable failure I was. But God—in the very middle of my self-accusation—interrupted me with words so clear and compelling that I can still take you to the exact spot where I was standing when he spoke! What did he say? He simply said, "I will be a Father to you." I protested, of course, pointing out again: "You don't understand, God, I am a failure!" And Papa said in reply, "No, you don't understand! I will be a Father to you." The significance of those words cannot be overstated. Because of father wounds related to fear of failure (I never measured up), I had *never* been able to think of God as Father. But something was healed in me that day, and that was the beginning of my journey into the Father's heart. (He also completely redeemed the situation, but that's a story for another time.)

I hope you catch the wonder and grace in this story. The truth is that I had failed miserably, and

God would have been justified in rebuking me. Instead, because he knew what I really needed to hear, he changed my world forever with words I had longed all my life to hear. I have many, many stories like this. I think of the first time I heard God say, "I am proud of you." Again, I can take you to the place where I was standing and speak volumes about how that healed me.

Response

What about you? Think about what God's voice tends to sound like when you hear him. Take time to shift your perspective, if needed, and "install new filters" for what you are sensing God saying to you. Be sure to make a plan to check in with trusted friends, too, if you need help determining if what you are hearing sounds like Papa.

NOTES

17 Papa

Hides Things for Our Good

*"My thoughts are not your thoughts,
neither are your ways my ways," declares
the Lord. "As the heavens are higher
than the earth, so are my ways higher
than your ways and my thoughts than
your thoughts." – Isaiah 55:8–9*

I sat in disbelief as the gifted and passionate teacher of God's Word told us why she so strongly disliked Isaiah 55:8–9. Her reason? She believed that the things God kept hidden from us referred to the bad things that happen in life! God's higher thoughts and ways in her mind referred to the hard things that so often cause us to ask "Why, God?"

But I also smiled as I listened to her words because of something Father had previously shown me about his mysterious ways through this passage. Like many others, I took this passage to mean something like, "Listen, Tom, your pea brain just can't get it, so when things that you don't like and you don't understand happen, just suck it up. After all, God's ways are just too far beyond yours." Well, okay, maybe not everyone thinks like that or puts it that bluntly, but we *do* seem to think that the bad things that happen are somehow part of God's mysterious ways and that we just have to buck up. But when God opened my eyes about this passage, he led me to an astounding discovery: *Mystery* in the New Testament is, with perhaps one exception, always about something *good* that God is revealing about himself! (Check it out for yourself by searching on *mystery* in the New Testament.)

This passage in Isaiah also reveals this truth in living color. Check out the two verses that immediately precede vv. 8–9:

> Seek the Lord while he may be found;
> call on him while he is near.

Let the wicked forsake his ways

and the unrighteous their thoughts.

Let them turn to the Lord, *and he will have mercy on them,*

and to our God, *and he will freely pardon.*

"For my thoughts are not your thoughts."

– vv. 6–8, emphasis mine

Do you see what I saw? The exalted, unsearchable thoughts of God are in the context of his mercy toward those (rebellious people) who turn toward him. In other words, it's about his goodness! What is mysterious about God is not the fact that bad things happen in this world but that he is so very, very good! He is so astonishingly good and loving and kind that the best human definitions of these traits fall infinitely short, because his thoughts are not our thoughts, and our ways are not like his! When God has something up his sleeve that we can't understand, we can be sure that it's something good, not something bad.

What does this mean for me? For you? Well, for me it has changed my entire perspective about life and how God is working in the midst of life. Now, no matter what happens (and I have been in some very, very hard times), I find myself looking for evidence of his amazing, totally good—if mysterious—will. As I realize that he is so beyond my best thoughts and operates for my good in ways so far beyond my ways, I am stunned. And I am loved into surrender, restfulness, and yes, even expectancy.

So when God hides something, what he is hiding is just too good to be fully understood at the present time. No wonder, then, that Paul, when writing of the unsearchable things of God, put it in the context of God's astonishing mercy:

> For God has bound all men over to disobedience so that he may have *mercy* on them all.
>
> Oh, the depth of the riches of the wisdom and knowledge of God!
>
> How unsearchable his judgments,
>
> and his paths beyond tracing out!
>
> "Who has known the mind of the Lord?
>
> Or who has been his counselor?"
>
> "Who has ever given to God,
>
> that God should repay him?"
>
> For from him and through him and to him are all things.
>
> To him be the glory forever! Amen.
>
> – Romans 11:32–36, emphasis added

Response

How does it change things for you to think about God hiding things for your good? Write a few thoughts about how this can change your view of the inexplicably bad things that happen in life and in our world. Consider, too, what it means that God might have really good surprises up his sleeve. What does a world look like that has the God of good surprises always at work?

NOTES

18 PAPA IS FAITHFUL

I will sing of the Lord's great love forever;
with my mouth I will make your
faithfulness known through all
generations. I will declare that your love
stands firm forever, that you established
your faithfulness in heaven itself.
— Psalm 89:1–2

For great is your love, higher than the
heavens; your faithfulness reaches to the
skies. — Psalm 108:4

I have been overwhelmed by God's faithfulness more times in my life than I can count. Actually, I pretty much *remain* overwhelmed by his faithfulness. Like Ethan, author of Psalm 89, I am compelled to make God's faithfulness known; like David in Psalm 108, my life reveals that God's love and faithfulness stretch beyond the skies.

God's faithfulness, an expression of his love, invites us into ever-deepening trust in him. Biblical faith is relational: it is the growing trust that develops between persons as they get to know one another. There is, then, a deep connection between God's trustworthiness and our trust (faith).

Why is this important to know? Because it helps a great deal to redefine faith as a beautiful expression of trust from the heart instead of a head thing. But sadly, faith for some people is more a reactionary attempt to believe God's promises than a heart response of trust in a loving, trustworthy God. When distress comes to someone with this mindset, they try to build their faith instead of responding with the confident expectancy *already in them* through their many encounters with God's trustworthiness. But as we realize that the God journey is about relationship, the thought of building our faith becomes irrelevant. In fact, it becomes counterproductive because it shifts our focus away from the relationship. God's design is for our faith to be always growing deeper as we get to know him as the One whose faithfulness stretches to the skies.

Papa God is inviting you today to open your eyes to the countless expressions of his faithfulness in your life. As you do so, you will, more and more, walk with him with the simple expectancy of a little child in ever-growing trust.

This quote in *Divine Healing: A Scriptural Approach to Sickness, Faith, and Healing* (Andrew Murray, Createspace, 2013, p. 39) expresses this well:

> We would insist here that faith is not a logical reasoning which ought in some way to oblige God to act according to His promises. It is rather the confiding attitude of the child who honors his Father, who counts upon His love to see Him fulfilling His promises, and who knows that He is faithful to communicate to the body as well as to the soul the new strength which flows from the redemption, until the moment of departure is come.

Wow, so faith is not something that I "use" to get God "to behave" but the trusting expectancy of a child who really knows his Father!

There's also this in *The Shack* (Wm. Paul Young, Newbury Park, CA: Windblown Media, 2008, p. 127):

> "The real underlying flaw in your life, Mackenzie, is that you don't think that I am good. If you knew I was good and that everything—the means, the ends, and all the processes of individual lives—is all

covered by my goodness, then while you might not always understand what I am doing, you would trust me."

"Mackenzie, you cannot produce trust just like you cannot 'do' humility. It either is or is not. Trust is the fruit of a relationship in which you know you are loved. Because you do not know that I love you, you *cannot* trust me."

Response

So what now? Here's a few suggestions for you. First, do a search on *faithfulness* in the Bible, then reflect on what you discover. Second, to help combat the westernized version of faith, take every place in the New Testament where you read "believe," and translate it "trust." You will be amazed at how this one little adjustment changes things for you. Third, take some time to thank God for specific times you have seen his goodness and faithfulness in your life.

NOTES

19 PAPA

KEEPS HIS PROMISES

*By faith even Sarah, who was past
childbearing age, was enabled to bear
children because she considered him
faithful who had made the promise.*
— Hebrews 11:11 NIV

One of the things I wrestled most with after my Jettie died was the confusion I felt because of all the promises of healing that Jettie and I (and many others) heard God giving to us. Did God change his mind or just plain old "fib" to us? Did we hear God so poorly that we missed the obvious warnings that death was coming? I am convinced that the answer is *absolutely not!* God *did* promise to heal. Because he always wants to heal, what else could we expect him to say? (Jesus healed all who came to him. See Acts 10:38.) So even when God knows we aren't in a place of faith to move the mountains of sickness, he promises to heal because that promise has already been made in the Bible.

I also believe that God, like any good parent, is always urging us to go beyond where he knows we will get. We parents know how this works: we encourage our kids at a very early age to reach beyond their capacity. For example, when they begin to walk, we deliberately get farther away than they may be able to reach, all the while saying, "Come on, you can make it!" So when God's people face mountains of opposition, even if he knows that this time the mountain won't move, he will still say, "Come on, you can trust me for this one!"

One great example occurred when Jesus invited Peter to walk on water, knowing very well that Peter would need rescuing. Instead of saying to Peter, "You can't make it; you will sink about halfway," he said, "Come!" He then rescued Peter from Peter's failure of faith. I think this is what happened in the battle for Jettie's healing. Even though God knew that our trust level wasn't able to receive his power to heal, he urged us on, ready to catch us and redeem the situation when we fell. After all, Jettie is certainly better off by far, and even in the indescribable pain of those of us left behind, God's presence is doing remarkable things.

But does this leave me feeling like a failure? It did at first, of course, and possibly will again, but Papa has quickly corrected any notion that I am responsible for the impossible. That's his realm. Instead, in the safety of his constant loving embrace, he invites me to get to know him better than ever so that the next time, faith (trust) will lay hold of his promises more fully than ever.

So I grieved; oh, how I grieved! For a while it hurt beyond my ability to describe (Jettie and I had a remarkably good marriage, and she was my best and most treasured friend). But even in my grief, through the massive confusion, I heard the invitation to get to know him ringing in my heart louder than ever. And I still hear that invitation. What else can I do, then, except pursue him even through the pain? That is what I will do, holding more tightly to his promises than ever.

Response

Do you have promises in your life that you feel God didn't keep? If so, I recommend asking God to forgive you for doubting his character. God is the ultimate promise keeper and never lies or breaks a promise. Next, why not renew some solid promises God has made to you in light of any new insight from today's chapter? Also, read Hebrews 11, and wrestle a bit with these words from the unknown author of this letter: "All these people earned a good reputation because of their faith, yet none of them received all that God had promised. For God had something better in mind for us, so that they would not reach perfection without us" (vv. 39–40 NLT).

NOTES

20 PAPA

GOD IS ABOVE TIME

See, the former things have taken place,
and new things I declare; before they
spring into being I announce them to
you.
— Isaiah 42:9

Before time began, God always was. After time ends, God always will be. There was never a time when God was not, and there will never be a time when God will not be. He encompasses all of time within himself and then goes on beyond it forever.

Because Papa contains time within himself, it's easy for him to tell us anything he chooses about future events (he is already there in the future, just as he is always in the past). In fact, in more than one place, Isaiah cites God's ability to foretell the future as one of the marks of his "Godness."

Is this giving you a headache or making you say so what? I hope not, because thoughts like this will bring a sense of worship and awe to us that take us out of ourselves into a place of holy fear. God's eternal nature, and the omniscience that flows from it, reveals the *infinite* gulf between Creator and creature that Papa spanned to reconcile us to himself. And we are undone! I tremble as I write this.

But there is also amazing comfort for us in God's being above time. For example, God's sovereignty allows him to work out everything according to his purpose without violating the free will of his creatures. And his promise to work everything out for the good of those who love him brings us comfort even when evil seems to be winning the day. Because he knows the end from the beginning, God is able to work in the background so that even the (infinitely-stupider-than-God) enemy's worst works will be turned to good in the end. I don't understand how all this will happen, nor does any creature he has made, but as one who has stood in the rubble of tragedy, personally and with many others, I take great comfort in knowing that God is above time and, therefore, able to "use" time to work out his perfect, perfectly loving purposes.

Another wonderful implication of God containing time within himself occurs when he takes us back to something in the past to encourage us in the present moment. I had one of those moments this morning. I was in need of very specific encouragement about some very specific things in a very specific way. Papa's answer was to nudge me to go back exactly eleven months in my journal to read what I had written there. When I did, I was blown away to see *exactly* the *specific* encouragement I needed in *exactly* the *specific* form I needed it. I could write much more about this (there were many, many God coincidences connected with this event), but suffice it to say that only a God who knows everything could have orchestrated this. And God has done this for me countless times!

I smile as I think of what he said to me when I asked him how he does this. I sensed his laughter as he said, "It's easy when you know everything!" I smile even now as I think of that. What wonder and love is this, that an infinite God would bend his infiniteness to bless his very finite creatures?

Ah, Papa, we are undone by your kindness and by your impossible-to-grasp power and knowledge!

Response

Pray this prayer with me today: "God above time, we worship you even as we realize how our remembering this truth assures us that you can and will reveal things to us whenever we need them. You can, at any moment, as needed, drop into our listening spirits whatever we need to know so that we can best serve others! Keep us listening, then, God above time, that your kingdom may come and your will be done on earth as it is in heaven."

NOTES

21 PAPA

GOD IS SOVEREIGN

*He makes everything work out according
to his plan. – Ephesians 1:11 NLT*

*And we know that God causes everything
to work together for the good of those
who love God and are called according to
his purpose for them.
– Romans 8:28 NLT*

Nothing seems stranger to me than the statement that God somehow *causes* the death of someone we love (e.g., "God just needed her in heaven."). God is depicted as pulling levers to cause everything that happens in life, good or bad. This simply isn't true! God may be in control, but not like that! That road ends up with a god who kills babies in the womb, kills children, causes war, and so on. But death and evil were not God's idea nor his plan for us, not originally and not ever. A god who directly causes everything is not the God of the Bible. The God of Scripture is sovereign, but he doesn't *make* everything happen. That view of God is called *determinism* and is *not* the God we meet in Scripture.

God's sovereignty means that he causes everything that happens to fit into his ultimate purpose (Ephesians 1:11; Romans 8:28–29). God granted freedom of choice to his creatures so that genuine relationship with him would be possible. Relationships require freedom of choice because they can't be coerced. You may submit to a dictator, but you won't have a loving relationship with him! Ability to choose relationship with God includes the ability *not* to choose the relationship, and that required freedom has resulted in a world where really bad choices continue to give birth to terribly evil things. But Papa is also always working redemptively (often invisibly) to cause everything to work out for his ultimate good purpose: the revelation of his infinite love and goodness (his

glory). Who can understand how God does this?
It's obvious that many things happen that aren't his
will, yet everything will somehow be folded into his
overall, eternal purpose in the end. (My head hurts
as I write this.)

Furthermore, our being created in God's image
requires us to be free, as God is, to choose good.
Only when we *choose* to be good are we really good
(like our Father). Forced goodness is not goodness
at all. Love (the motivation behind goodness)
cannot be forced, and nothing is more like Papa
God than love. Wow! So even our being created in
God's image means that evil is a possibility, because
free choice allows for it. So although God never
chooses evil, the power of choice given to his
creatures has, sadly, often resulted in evil. But
again, we find that our loving Father will redeem
everything in the end so that all will once again be
very good.

I can love and trust a God like that! Common
sense tells us that we can't be in a loving, trusting
relationship with a god who causes anything bad.
Who could love a god who hurts us for his glory or
who might do something but chooses instead to do
nothing for his glory? But knowing that God is
good—absolutely and completely good—enables us
to keep trusting him *even when we don't understand*
the evil that's happening.

Picture God's purpose as a huge river, flowing
to a distant, beautiful destination. Everything in

time and creation is being carried along on that river, and people (and other creatures) in the river have freedom to do whatever they wish while being carried along in its flow. They can bump into one another, fight the flow, move with the flow, go from side to side, but they cannot escape being carried along with the river to the final destination. This isn't a perfect picture, but it helps me, and maybe it will help you. There is a river of God's purpose, flowing through time and eternity, that carries everything along to a good end, even while it allows perfect freedom within the context of its flow. I choose to rest in that river, even when things bump into me or even submerge me for a while along the way!

Response

Write down your reflections about this conversation from *The Shack* (p. 185):

> Papa to Mack: "Mack, just because I work incredible good out of unspeakable tragedies doesn't mean I orchestrate the tragedies. Don't ever assume that my using something means that I caused it or that I need it to accomplish my purposes. That will only lead you to false notions about me. Grace doesn't depend on suffering to exist, but where there is suffering you will find grace in many facets and colors."

NOTES

22 Papa Is All Powerful

One thing God has spoken, two things I have heard: "Power belongs to you, God, and with you, Lord, is unfailing love"; and, "You reward everyone according to what they have done."
– Psalm 62:11–12

I stood in stunned wonder as I watched people being healed all over the room. The healings were spontaneous, numerous, and remarkably clear demonstrations of God's power. I was with Gary Oates and a large team on a trip to Joinville, Brazil, and before Gary even started speaking, the Holy Spirit came upon the people in the room. It was as if waves of joy and power were sweeping through the room, and as the waves came, people were being healed.

The power of God continued when our teams finally stood to minister healing. I cannot remember all the testimonies, but I remember hearing stories of a woman's deaf ear being opened, of another older woman's blind eye receiving back its sight, of a man with AIDS being healed, and more. I remember demons fleeing with a word, as I and others addressed them, and people collapsing under the weight of God's healing presence. It was amazing, and I smile even twelve years later as I reflect on what I witnessed.

I have seen many instances of God's power working like this—yes, even here in the United States. One men's retreat comes to mind as we saw three creative miracles in one night—one of which caused a young man's arm to grow about five inches as his stunned friends watched in amazement. Papa God is all powerful!

Scriptures confirm over and over that God is all powerful and that his power is at work in us and available to us. Consider just a few passages (in addition to the one quoted above):

> Because he loved your fathers, he chose their descendants after them and brought you out of Egypt by his presence and great power. (Deuteronomy 4:37 CSB)

> Great is our Lord and mighty in power; his understanding has no limit. (Psalm 147:5)

> Oh, Lord God! You yourself made the heavens and earth by your great power and with your outstretched arm. Nothing is too difficult for you! (Jeremiah 32:17 CSB)

> For nothing will be impossible with God. (Luke 1:37 CSB)

> I pray that the eyes of your heart may be enlightened so that you may know what is the hope of his calling, what is the wealth of his glorious inheritance in the saints, and what is the immeasurable greatness of his power toward us who believe, according to the mighty working of his strength. (Ephesians 1:18–19 CSB)

But if all this is true, why don't we see his power like this all the time? After all, I am writing this as one whose first wife died from cancer despite thousands of prayers on her behalf. Is God capricious or moody in the display of his power? Not at all! In fact, I have heard Jesus say more than once amid power demonstrations, "This is who I really am, little one. I AM always like this!" So more than ever, I choose not to water down

Scripture to fit my experience but rather to live in expectancy as I wait for Papa to display his power.

Response

Take some time today to reflect on *The Passion Translation* rendering of Ephesians 1:19–20:

> I pray that you will continually experience the immeasurable greatness of God's power made available to you through faith. Then your lives will be an advertisement of this immense power as it works through you! This is the mighty power that was released when God raised Christ from the dead and exalted him to the place of highest honor and supreme authority in the heavenly realm!

What do you hear God saying to you about his power? Where in your life and in the world around you do you need to say to God, "Show your power, oh God!"? Ask Papa to make the prayer in Ephesians 1:19–20 a regular appeal from your heart, then watch what he does!

NOTES

23 Papa Is Eager to Show Us His Ways

Show me your ways, Lord, teach me your paths. Guide me in your truth and teach me, for you are God my Savior, and [I wait in expectancy for] you all day long.
– Psalm 25:4–5

Interesting, isn't it, that the Bible never says we should ask God to teach us principles or show us his doctrines? A while ago, as I reflected on what was happening in my life during the battle for Jettie's life, I became more convinced than ever that we must think of our relationship with God as far more than theology, doctrine, and principles.

I've had lots of conversations with God about this. I invite you now to listen in on this one from my journal, dated July 30, 2011:

Ah, Father. I will trust in you!

"Child, I have been showing you these past few days how trustworthy I am, how generous and kind I am. I am gracious and generous and wanting to show you my ways, the riches of my kindness, so that you can enter into this next season. And I will succeed in my intentions, little one. Yes, even now you can glimpse (if but barely) what will be radiantly apparent for you in just a little while. My goodness is coming upon you, child, more than you can imagine or bear. I will smother you with grace and shower you with kindness over and over until you get it. Then, yes, then, you will trust me in an unprecedented manner!

> Taste and see, indeed, little one, that I
> am good—very, very, very good!"
>
> Ah, Papa. I do indeed glimpse things, if but
> barely, but I seem unable at this point to
> hold on to what I see. But you will change
> that, I know. Open my eyes! Show me your
> ways!

Do you see Papa's kindness in this conversation? His persistent kindness is how we learn what faith really looks like, as I have already said many times in this little book. Even human relationships teach us this: It isn't just *knowing* that a friend *might* help me that causes me to trust him or her. And it isn't just knowing *about* a friend's supportiveness to other people that invites me to trust him or her. No, it's my *actual experience* of that friend's help that invites and increases my trust. Learning to trust Papa God is no different. That's why David (and others) cried out to God to know *his* ways, to learn *his* paths. They weren't asking this to have something to do or an example to copy. They wanted to know, *by experience,* the truly trustworthy One.

"Yes, Papa, show us *your* ways, teach us *your* paths! They are precious to us, not because they work for us but because they express your heart and invite us to ever-deeper trust. We love who you are, Papa!"

Response

Much of "Christianity" seems to get lost in complicated and convoluted facts, principles, and proof texts. For me, though, I will again and again prepare a path that invites others into Papa's heart. How about you? Does your heart crave facts or a Father's embrace? Do you long for more principles or for more of his presence and truth (his faithfulness, not facts about him)? Consider changing your thinking today about standing on the promises by shifting your position of being embraced by the Promise-Giver!

NOTES

24 Papa

Longs to Be Your One Thing

You shall love the Lord your God with all your heart and with all your soul and with all your might.
— Deuteronomy 6:5 (ESV)

"*Am* I your one thing, little one?" Papa's voice broke into my reflections about One Thing. Wow! I was undone, and I am still pondering, my heart reaching toward God in invitation and appeal: Please, Papa, become so precious to me that I can't help but say, "Yes, Lord God, you are my one thing!"

There is a beautiful thread woven throughout the Bible related to God as our One Thing. One of the first places is in the life of Enoch, who made God his One Thing so much that one day God invited him directly into his eternal presence (Genesis 5:24). In Deuteronomy, we hear God's invitation to make loving him our One Thing: "Love the Lord your God with all your heart and with all your soul and with all your strength" (Deuteronomy 6:5 ESV). This is added to with the words, "Man does not live on bread alone but on every word that comes from the mouth of the Lord" (Deuteronomy 8:3). The One Thing theme swells to a powerful high point in David's declaration: "One thing I ask of the Lord, this is what I seek: that I may dwell in the house of the Lord all the days of my life, to gaze upon the beauty of the Lord and to seek him in his temple" (Psalm 27:4).

In the New Testament, Jesus—as we would expect—lived the perfect One-Thing life. His life was completely consumed with love for, and dependence upon, his Abba. "I tell you the truth, the Son can do nothing by himself. He does only what he sees the Father doing" (John 5:19 NLT). His life was completely focused on his Father's face so that he never missed a single loving glance nor a single moment of his Father's purposes. Jesus invited others to live the One-Thing life, most notably in his words to Martha and Mary: "Few things are needed—or indeed only one. Mary has chosen what is better, and it will not be taken away from her" (Luke 10:42 NIV).

The apostle Paul also lived the One-Thing life and invited others to imitate him in it: "But one thing I do: Forgetting what is behind and straining toward what is ahead, I press on toward the goal to win the prize for which God has called me heavenward in Christ Jesus" (Philippians 3:13–14). Is Paul's One Thing the same as elsewhere in Scripture? Yes. He defines his One Thing a few verses earlier: "I want to know Christ" (Philippians 3:10).

It was all this I was pondering this morning, with a sense of wonder at the incredible life that God has invited us to live in, a life blinded to anything else, anyone else, except him—a life so consumed with God and his goodness that he cannot be anything other than our One Thing. We are held captive not by our willpower but by his sheer, overpowering, persistent goodness!

He once again breaks into my reverie: "*Am I your one thing, little one?*" I am so undone!

Response

Take some time to reflect on the lives of David, Paul, and Jesus, asking yourself this question: What do I see in their lives that gives me clues about how they discovered and lived the One-Thing life? As you do this, I recommend putting the focus not so much on what they did or did not do but on what Father God did. Write down a few discoveries, and let them seep deeply into your heart, as you cry out to Papa to increase your hunger for him above all others.

NOTES

RESPONDING TO PAPA

I have supplied some suggested responses to Papa in each day's entry, but for these last few days, I want to be more intentional about how to respond to our amazing Papa. The Bible makes it clear in more than one place that change happens only when we respond—merely agreeing won't change a thing.

So, everyone who hears these words of mine and acts on them will be like a sensible man who built his house on bedrock. The rain fell, the rivers flooded, the winds blew and beat against that house, but it didn't collapse, because its foundation was on rock. But everyone who hears these words of mine and does not act on them will be like a stupid man who built his house on sand. The rain fell, the rivers flooded, the wind blew and beat against that house, and it collapsed — and its collapse was horrendous!

– Matthew 7:24–27 CJB

Don't just listen to the Word of Truth and not respond to it, for that is the essence of self-deception. So always let his Word become like poetry written and fulfilled by your life! If you listen to the Word and don't live out the message you hear, you become like the person who looks in the mirror of the

Word to discover the reflection of his face in the beginning. You perceive how God sees you in the mirror of the Word, but then you go out and forget your divine origin. But those who set their gaze deeply into the perfecting law of liberty are fascinated by and respond to the truth they hear and are strengthened by it—they experience God's blessing in all that they do!

– James 1:22–25 TPT

Respond we must, if we wish to be truly changed. There is no limit to the ways we can respond to an infinitely amazing God, of course, but consider the following as possible first steps.

25 LET

PAPA DEFINE LOVE

This is love: not that we loved God, but that he loved us and sent his Son as an atoning sacrifice for our sins.
— 1 John 4:10

Many of us as children probably said more than once, "If you *really* loved me, you would …" (Or if we are parents, we have heard it from our children!) As I have watched God demonstrate his love for us in very special ways over the years, I have also realized that I *still* say that to him sometimes, but trying to tell God what his love should look like is a dead-end road! In fact, anytime I find myself questioning God's love for me because it doesn't look or feel like love, I know I am already heading down that dead-end road.

For love to be freely and properly expressed, God as our lover must be the one who defines what love looks like and how it is expressed. There are a number of reasons for that, of course—sometimes even in the realm of human love—but it's especially true in terms of God's love for us. Consider the following:

- If I decide how God is supposed to express his love for me, I will miss many, *if not most,* of his expressions of love for me simply because my "filter" prevents me from seeing his love.

- Since love is about receiving and trusting and surrendering, if I am the one who defines what love looks like, I am the one in control, and my control blocks my capacity to receive what God is freely offering me.

- In God's case, he alone knows how best to express his love for us. Our limited ability to

127

see, understand, and the like, keeps us from having any real clue as to what we *really* need. God, however, in his perfect love and "Godness," *always* sees *everything* so that he can always do what is best for us (He really is a GOOD FATHER). So, let's see, who do I *really* want defining what love looks like?

I remember to this day how odd it felt for my sons to question our love for them (which, thankfully, they didn't do very often). Jettie and I knew that we loved them without limit and that we were always seeking to do what was best for them. How odd, then, for them to question that. How much odder and foolish it is, then, for me to question the love of the perfect parent! May God help us all to start with God. Is. Love. From that firm beginning, we will be able to live lives that allow *him* to define and express his love as he knows best. Living from this perspective will open new experiences of his love in thousands of ways. His love will explode onto the scenes of our lives in ways that stagger us with the sheer magnitude of their goodness and power!

"Thank you, Papa, that you are the One who defines love, not I! Thank you for adjusting my heart as needed when I think otherwise. Grant me grace to turn quickly back to you as the One who is love when my thoughts begin to demand what love must look like."

Response

Ephesians 3:17–19 is a perfect prayer response to today's thoughts: "I pray that you, being rooted and established in love, may have power, together with all the Lord's holy people, to grasp how wide and long and high and deep is the love of Christ, and to know [by experience] this love that surpasses knowledge—that you may be filled to the measure of all the fullness of God!" Take a moment to ask Holy Spirit if there are "filters" you need to remove—things that have blinded you to Papa's love. Take some time, too, to consider how you can, more firmly than ever, start from the unshakeable foundation of "God loves me, period!"

NOTES

26

RESPOND TO PAPA
AS THE GREAT
INITIATOR (PART 1)

*No one can come to me unless the Father
who sent me draws them, and I will raise
them up at the last day.*
– John 6:44

We have made it clear, I trust, that the foundation of intimacy with Papa is knowing him as he really is and that he is better and "gooder" than we could ever imagine. Discovering how good he really is changes how we relate to him. For me, when I first began to realize this, it felt like everything I'd thought about God needed to be turned upside down for me to really get to know him.

One example of this occurred the day I realized I was the pursued rather than the pursuer. At some point in my hot pursuit of God, I stopped trying so hard to catch him, and he crashed into me! I discovered that *He* is the initiator and I am the responder.

Beginning with Adam's fall ("Adam, where are you?"), and continuing throughout the Bible, it is God who is the initiator: Abraham was worshiping idols and not looking for God, Moses was tending sheep and not looking for God, David was tending sheep and certainly not planning to be king of Israel, Simon and Andrew were cleaning their nets and not planning to be two of the Twelve, and Saul of Tarsus was *certainly not* planning to become a follower of Jesus! The entire redemption story is all about God pursuing his wandering children and paying an infinite price to reconcile them to himself (Romans 5:6–8; 2 Corinthians 5:18–19). Papa is, without a doubt, the great initiator.

This changes everything! If God is the pursuer, then my focus is shifted from trying to trusting, from running to resting, from moving to being still. My viewpoint shifts from watching what *I* am doing and how *I* am doing it to gazing at the One I want to meet and listening for his voice.

This gets even better as it dawns on us that we've been *chasing what we already have.* Believers are *already* in Christ, *already* seated in the heavenly realms, *already* hidden with Christ in God, *already* face-to-face with God, *already* indwelt by God the Holy Spirit—and on and on it goes. Discovering this truth for me was like returning home after another hard day of pursuing God only to find that he was there waiting for me in the living room!

Does this mean that we must wait helplessly until God decides to initiate things in our lives? Not at all. He *is* the initiator, but we must *respond* to his invitations. He *is* pursuing us, but we need to *respond* to the Pursuer. It's a different kind of response and not at all a self-focused activity. It's powered by a different motivation. It's about discovery rather than frantic effort. The following thoughts from early in the journey reveal my own awe and wonder at how my paradigms were changing. I pray that something about these words will help you respond to the great Initiator as he pursues you.

July 3, 2004, the day after my first intimacy encounter with Papa:

Can we, can I, Abba, hope to have a relationship with you like Moses: face-to-face? Surely the answer is yes, and for all believers, not just a few. Second Corinthians 3:7–18 seems to indicate that we all can have unveiled, face-to-face intimacy with you. . . .

Abba, what have we been missing?!! We have feared subjectivity and error so much that we have cut out the heart of what Jesus died to give us: true face-to-face, communication-filled intimacy with you!

But my heart sings at what I am starting to see. Show me all that you choose, Abba!

The implications of this are huge! We have inadvertently—with good intentions—cut out the heart of the good news. No wonder your people are burdened and powerless. No wonder they resort to legalism. They think that they are alone! For most of us, walking in the Spirit means filling our minds with Scripture, then hoping that we will guess what you are saying. But now I see, Abba.

Response

Does thinking of God being in hot pursuit of you change anything about how you view him? Take some time to reflect and give thanks for the many times God has very obviously pursued you to bless you, love on you, and invite you into his embrace.

NOTES

27

RESPOND TO PAPA
AS THE GREAT INITIATOR (PART 2)

*God demonstrates his own love for us in
this: While we were still sinners, Christ
died for us.*
— Romans 5:8

Day 27

In day 26, I wrote about how truly and fiercely loving and stubbornly pursuing Papa is. As we get this, our actions shift from being powered by frantic desperation to confident, expectant desire. We are stirred to go to any lengths to find Papa, but it's more like we're waiting in ambush for the God we know is already after us! We are waiting expectantly for a loving Daddy rather than chasing unsuccessfully after a rather disinterested God who plays hide-and-seek.

The behavior that flows from this healthy motivation is more focused and intense than behavior motivated by fear. Fearful motivation *(I hope he loves me. If I can just make him love me …)* will never lead to a healthy relationship with Papa because we are attempting to build a relationship with someone *who does not exist.* Our hearts cannot fully embrace One we fear more than we love or trust. On the other hand, if I know that I know that I know that I will find infinite love waiting for me, I will joyfully and passionately pursue my Pursuer, and this opens the door to intimacy beyond comprehension. We can forever drown in the depths of his love—there is no end, not ever! Song of Songs 3:4 (TPT) captures some of this passion: "I found the one I adore! I caught him and fastened myself to him, refusing to be feeble in my heart again."

It changes everything for us to *really know* that God is the initiator, fiercely chasing us down so he can be good to us and love on us. One thing that

138

has helped me get this is Papa's reminders of the love-infused times I had with my own sons. Jon, Josh, and I have enjoyed many fun and love-filled times together: walks on the beach, going fishing, wrestling on the floor, and much, much more. Papa also reminds me of times when my love was fierce and aggressive: I once rushed down a hill to pluck Josh out of an anthill. Nothing could have stopped me from reaching him! I smile as I write those words: I remember how hesitant my sons were to tell me about anyone messing with them, because they knew how fiercely I would protect them. Yes, my sons knew that I was fierce and unrelenting in my love for them (I still am), and God has used that truth to show me how to respond to him. He reminds me that he is infinitely more loving and fiercer in his love for me than I could ever be toward my sons. I can't imagine a love stronger than my love for my sons, but Papa's love for me, for you, is infinitely greater!

I don't write as one who has all this totally mastered. I still sometimes catch myself thinking of God as distant or deliberately making things hard on me! The good news is that he still comes after me (us) while I hold a faulty perspective or attitude. He is ever the pursuer.

Thank you, Papa, that even when I wander or lose sight of your goodness, you continue to pursue me and initiate good things for me and in me! And when I see this with renewed clarity, how else can I respond to you except to always return to your embrace the moment I see you?

Response

Consider how you will respond to the great Initiator in light of this passionate passage of Scripture:

> I've made up my mind.
>
> Until the darkness disappears and the dawn has fully come,
>
> in spite of shadows and fears,
>
> I will go to the mountaintop with you—
>
> the mountain of suffering love
>
> and the hill of burning incense.
>
> Yes, I will be Your bride.
>
> – Song of Songs 4:6 TPT

NOTES

28 Run Toward Papa's Smile

It was not our fathers' swords that took the land. It was not their strong arms that brought them victory. It was your power. It was because you accepted them and smiled down on them.
— Psalm 44:3 ERV

It started with a footnote, two little lines at the end of Psalm 16 as translated by Brian Simmons in *The Passion Translation*. Here's what it said: "There is no Hebrew word for 'presence.' When the psalmist wanted to speak of God's presence, he used the word for 'face.'"

It's hard to describe what happened to me as I read those words, but one thing for sure is that I was drawn into a deeper place of intimacy with Papa as I meditated on the difference between the rather impersonal sounding "presence of God" and the much more intimate sounding "face of God." I thought of one of the theme passages of my life, Exodus 33:14–15, and how different it sounds to read it when we hear God saying, "My face will go with you, and I will give you rest," and then to read Moses's response as "If we can't see your face, don't send us up from here."

I thought of some of the lyrics to the Paul Wilbur song, "Show Me Your Face," which talk about asking the Lord to show us his face but to give us enough strength to stand in his holy presence when he does. In difficult times, I sometimes have the thought that if I could just catch one glimpse of his face, it would be enough to wash away all doubt when it hits me.

And I thought of the chorus to a worship song I wrote a few years back, "Face-to-face":

> So we will run, we will hide, we will rest in your grace.

143

We will laugh, we will dance in your loving
embrace.

For you are willing, and you are waiting

To meet us face-to-face.

I thought, too, of the amazing truth that as a
believer my spirit is constantly gazing upon God's
face through the Holy Spirit. We really do live in
the constant state of meeting God face-to-face!

Papa showed me part of the significance of this
a while back as I watched our grandson Kai show
me how he could walk. I noticed something I'd
never caught before: as Kai walked into his daddy's
arms, he was looking intently at his daddy's smiling
face the entire time. Not once did he look at his
feet. Not once did he look at me to see if I was
watching. He simply ran toward his daddy's smile.

I wonder what it would be like to look at
Daddy's face and run towards Daddy's smile....

Response

How about you? Have you been looking at your feet
or gazing upon the smiling face of your Papa?
Consider how you will adjust your life to shift the
focus from doing things just right to dancing in
Papa's embrace. Consider how different it feels to
be motivated by a smile rather than by fear. Take a
moment, then, to glance at Papa's face and see his
smile, feel his embrace, hear his laughter.

NOTES

29 Build

Some Altars

The Lord appeared to Abram and said, "I will give this land to your offspring." So he built an altar there to the Lord who had appeared to him. From there he moved on to the hill country east of Bethel and … He built an altar to Yahweh there, and he called on the name of Yahweh.
– Genesis 12:7–8 HCSB

Many years ago, one of my college professors said, "You can tell where Abraham had been by the trail of altars he left behind." I have never forgotten that statement! Abraham marked his journey through life, especially all his major God-events, by building an altar (see Genesis 12:7–8; 13:4, 18; 22:9). His son Isaac and grandson Jacob did the same thing.

There is something profoundly healthy about building spiritual altars to mark major God-events in our lives. The New Testament's admonition to give thanks is an encouragement to look back at God's faithfulness and build altars of remembrance and gratitude.

Papa is always working in our lives, but there are times when he intersects them in a way that changes our course forever. Here are a few of my life-altering altar moments.

I was too young to know that I was building an altar during my first God encounter, but when I was about two or three years old, I had a powerful God encounter that set the course for the rest of my life. Papa awakened a God longing in me as I listened to a song my grandmother had given me, "God's Little Candles," by Hank Snow. I still remember my little heart longing for God as I listened to that song over and over. I call this altar the altar of First Longings. How amazing that God began to call me to himself before I even knew who was calling!

The next altar is the altar of Awakening. It was "built" during my first semester at Johnson Bible College. I was born from above that day after hearing Professor David Eubanks teach on 1 John 5:13, explaining that we can *know* that we have eternal life. To this day I can take you to the spot I was standing when "my heart was strangely warmed" (to quote John Wesley).

The third altar is an altar of Repentance. Dr. Eubanks lovingly but firmly confronted me about the terrible way I was treating my wife, Jettie. God's intervention through this gentle and courageous man literally saved my marriage, my future, my ministry, and my life! I weep with tears of gratitude as I visit this altar, built with stones of thanksgiving and awe-filled worship.

Another altar was created when I was twenty-two, and God in his kindness filled me with his Spirit—my first overwhelming encounter with him. I call this one the altar of Overwhelming. In his kindness, Papa held off answering my prayer to be filled with Holy Spirit until I had fully surrendered my marriage to him. Again, God's direct intervention was life altering and future shaping, not only because of the infusion of power that came into my life but also because of the deep repentance that he (again) brought into my life.

I have many more altars, of course: the births of my two sons, their marriages, the births of my grandchildren. So very many altars! But I close with just one more, the altar of Papa's Affirmation. I was standing outside of Calgary, Alberta, Canada, where I first heard God tell me he was proud of me. To understand the power of this moment, you need to know that I can't remember ever hearing those words from my dad or my mom, so when Papa interrupted my walk after a rather challenging inner healing session, I was completely unprepared for his words! I remember stopping in my tracks and checking to see if that really could be my Father. He assured me it was his voice, and he added the specific action and attitude of heart that he was affirming me for. I built an altar there.

These are but a few of the altars along the trail of my life. I trust that you realize these altars are about Papa, not me. My prayer, then, is that you see him more clearly in his love and grace as you gaze upon the now rather long trail of Tom's life and consider building a few altars yourself.

Response

Every follower of Jesus can build altars like these. Why not take some time today to build a few of your own in response to my trail of altars? If nothing else, ask Holy Spirit to help you make a list. I smile as I think of what will happen as you do!

NOTES

30 Make

the One Thing the One Thing

One thing I ask of the Lord,
this only do I seek: that I may dwell in
the house of the Lord all the days of my
life, to gaze on the beauty of the Lord and
to seek him in his temple.
— Psalm 27:4

DAY 30

The longer I live life with Jesus, the more convinced I am that life really can be as simple as the One-Thing life described on Day 24. If we can indeed make the main focus of our lives getting to know God ever more intimately—to gaze upon the beauty of the Lord, everything else will fall into place.

Too simple, you say? But have you really tried it? Have you asked God to create such hunger in you for him that nothing else will satisfy? Have you asked him to captivate you with his palpable presence so that like Moses you cry out, "If your Presence does not go with us, do not send us up from here" (Exodus 33:15)? Have you asked God to give you the kind of hunger for him that the sons of Korah describe: "As the deer pants for streams of water, so my soul pants for you, my God. My soul thirsts for God, for the living God" (Psalm 42)?

I could go on, but maybe you get my point. Many believers dismiss the simplicity of the One-Thing life because they have never experienced it, finding their lives distracted from the One Thing by serving like Martha (in Luke 10) or by the pursuit of lesser things like the wealthy ruler (Luke 18:18–23). I am not writing this to shame or pressure you, rather I invite you to ask God to create such hunger in you for him that nothing else but a God-transfixed, God-blinded, God-bathed life will do!

If you ask with a sincere heart, you will find Papa more than willing to begin drawing your heart to his, creating the same hunger in you that burned in David, Moses, Jesus, Paul, and many others. If you set your will to pursue this One-Thing life, trusting in his grace to create what is lacking in you (he is, after all, the Creator), you will be amazed at what happens. Admittedly, this won't happen overnight, but over the length of time that he knows is best, you will discover and begin to live out the simple intimacy of a One-Thing life.

Many of you already know and experience this, I am sure, so you know that some amazing things begin to happen in us as we live so simply and passionately. Faith grows ("fixing our eyes on Jesus, the pioneer and perfecter of faith" [Hebrews 12:2 NIV]). Shame and fear diminish ("Those who look to him are radiant; their faces are never covered with shame" [Psalm 34:5]). Our lives are transformed because we begin, more and more, to look like the One we are beholding ("We all, with unveiled faces, are looking as in a mirror at the glory of the Lord and are being transformed into the same image from glory to glory; this is from the Lord who is the Spirit" [2 Corinthians 3:18 HCSB]).

I am not writing about this as a theory. For over fifteen years I have been on the One-Thing journey. The journey has had some very unexpected and painful times as well as seasons of great joy and overwhelming wonder. And now, more than ever, I am convinced, through experience along with Scripture, that "only One Thing" is needed. I cannot tell you how my heart longs for you to experience this for yourself, dear one, but—and I am astonished at this thought—God's desire to give it to you is infinitely greater! May you hear clearly his persistent invitation.

Response

The title of today's devotion is "Make the One Thing the One Thing." Some of you, perhaps many or most of you, already live this out in your lives. For you, your response to all you have read may simply be, like mine, "More, Lord, more!" For some of you, though, today would be a great day to listen and respond to God's invitation to change whatever needs to be changed to live a One-Thing life. Take some time to write out a few thoughts on what that would look like in your life. What adjustments do you need to make to your schedule, what changes in your thinking, what things can you add? Who can be a partner with you in this to encourage you on the new journey? May your journey into Papa's heart be fuller and richer each day!

NOTES

A FINAL WORD

I began this journey by reminding you that you were created for an intimate relationship with the God of the universe—a truly remarkable thought! And it's even more remarkable that God has literally paid an immeasurable price to have that intimacy with you and is in hot pursuit of your heart every day of your life.

So where do you go from here? I pray that you will hear Papa's answer to that for yourself, but I also remind you of the following suggestions that have helped me in my journey into Papa's heart.

- Think relationship!
- Think encounter and experience, not just ideas.
- Think community—don't try to grow alone.
- Think solitude—don't lean on the community as a substitute for your personal relationship with God.
- Think restoration—inner healing is often part of the journey into intimacy.

- Think journey—any healthy relationship requires us to invest time and persist in our getting to know and learning to trust the other person.

- You may also find my thoughts on entering into intimacy on pages i–xi helpful.

Stop and turn around, my friend, and let Papa catch you! I know he will!

> I kneel humbly in awe before the Father of our Lord Jesus, the Messiah, the perfect Father of every father and child in heaven and on the earth. And I pray that he would unveil within you the unlimited riches of his glory and favor until supernatural strength floods your innermost being with his divine might and explosive power. Then, by constantly using your faith, the life of Christ will be released deep inside you, and the resting place of his love will become the very source and root of your life.
>
> Then you will be empowered to discover what every holy one experiences—the great magnitude of the astonishing love of Christ in all its dimensions. How deeply intimate and far-reaching is his love! How enduring and inclusive it is! Endless love beyond measurement that transcends our understanding—this extravagant love pours into you until you are filled to overflowing with the fullness of God!
>
> – Ephesians 3:14–19 TPT

WORKS CITED

WHO ARE YOU, PAPA?

Tozer, A.W. and Warren Wiersbe, *The Best of A. W. Tozer, Book One* (Pennsylvania: WingSpread, 2007).

DAY 1 AND DAY 18

Paul Young, *The Shack.* (Newbury Park, CA: Windblown Media, 2008).

DAY 4

Brother Lawrence, *The Practice of the Presence of God* (New York: Revell, 1895).

Amy Laura Hall. *Laughing at the Devil: Seeing the World with Julian of Norwich* (Durham: Duke University Press Books, 2018).

DAY 10

Andrew Murray, *With Christ in the School of Prayer* (New York: Fleming H. Revell, 1895).

DAY 18

Andrew Murray, *Divine Healing: A Scriptural Approach to Sickness, Faith, and Healing* (Createspace, 2013).

ABOUT TOM

Hi. This is where you usually read about accomplishments, degrees, etc. I am old enough to have a few of those, but here's what I think you should know about me:

I have been a follower of Jesus for more than fifty years. Like John Wesley, my heart was "strangely warmed" when I placed my trust in Jesus as Lord and Savior. I can still take you to the place where I was standing when that encounter with Jesus happened.

I am a husband, father, and grandpa. I am also a spiritual daddy to quite a few people, a truly humbling thing to me! I consider myself to be one of the least of Abba's children, yet I am able to say in clear conscience to any who wish to listen: Imitate Jesus as I imitate Him, love as I love, live as I live. The God I know and love is a God who is always speaking and who continues to work

159

supernaturally. His mission for me is to introduce as many as I can into intimate relationship with him.

My most important life markers, in my view, are related to my family: loving and supporting my wife, Charlie (and before Charlie, Jettie, for forty-one years, until she went to be with Jesus in October 2010). By God's grace, Jettie and I raised two sons, Jon and Josh, to love God with all their hearts, souls, and strength. Through my marriage to Charlie, God has added even more amazing family members to my life.

Tom

CONTACT TOM

FACEBOOK: www.facebook.com/tom.wymore

BLOG: www.tomwymore.blogspot.com

TWITTER: www.twitter.com/abbaslittleboy

TOM'S TEACHING MATERIALS

TOM'S MESSAGES: tinyurl.com/y8ygeaa8

TOM'S MESSAGE VIDEOS: tinyurl.com/y4j4jkx3

DIGGING DEEPER BIBLE STUDY 2019: tinyurl.com/yxfy88lk

PHILIPPIANS CLASS: tinyurl.com/yc9a96x5%20(

HEART OF ROMANS CLASS: tinyurl.com/y47g9h22

BIBLE STUDY CLASS 2017: tinyurl.com/y8nht3vs

EPHESIANS CLASS 2018: tinyurl.com/yaj27wqj

GALATIANS CLASS 2014: tinyurl.com/yxey3qyc

CAN YOU HELP?

Reviews are everything to an author, because they mean a book is given more visibility. If you enjoyed this book, please review it on your favorite book review sites and tell your friends about it. Thank you!

Made in the USA
Columbia, SC
09 November 2019